SELECTED POEMS OF HORACE GREGORY

by Horace Gregory

POETRY

Chelsea Rooming House
No Retreat
Chorus for Survival
Poems 1930–1940

PROSE

Pilgrim of the Apocalypse: A Study of D. H. Lawrence
The Shield of Achilles: Essays on Beliefs in Poetry
Samuel Johnson and the Metaphysical Poets
A History of American Poetry, 1900–1940
(in collaboration with Marya Zaturenska)

TRANSLATED BY HORACE GREGORY

The Poems of Catullus

EDITED BY HORACE GREGORY

New Letters in America
The Triumph of Life
The Portable Sherwood Anderson

Selected Poems.
of Horace Gregory

The Viking Press · New York · 1951

Printed in U.S.A. by The Vail-Ballou Press, Inc.

For Patrick Bolton Gregory

Hic quoque sit gratus parvus labor, ut tibi possim inde alios aliosque memor componere versus.

ACKNOWLEDGMENT

The author wishes to thank the editors of the following publications, in which a number of the poems included here made their first appearance: *Accent, Contemporary Poetry, Free World, The Harvard Advocate, Partisan Review, Poetry* (Chicago), *The Saturday Review of Literature, The Tiger's Eye,* and *Wake.* He also thanks Harcourt, Brace & Co. for permission to reprint certain poems which were published in *Poems 1930–1940,* included here in the sections called "Chelsea Rooming House," "No Retreat," "Chorus for Survival," "Fortune for Mirabel."

CONTENTS

I: CHELSEA ROOMING HOUSE

LONGFACE MAHONEY DISCUSSES HEAVEN

If someone said, Escape.
Let's get away from here,
you'd see snow mountains thrown
against the sky,
cold, and you'd draw your breath and feel
air like cold water going through your veins,
but you'd be free, up so high,
or you'd see a row of girls dancing on a beach
with tropic trees and a warm moon
and warm air floating under your clothes
and through your hair.
Then you'd think of heaven
where there's peace, away from here,
and you'd go someplace unreal
where everybody goes after something happens,
set up in the air, safe, a room in a hotel.
A brass bed, military hairbrushes,
a couple of coats, trousers, maybe a dress
on a chair or draped on the floor.
This room is not on earth, feel the air,
warm like heaven and far away.

This is a place
where marriage nights are kept
and sometimes here you say Hello
to a neat girl with you
and sometimes she laughs

because she thinks it's funny to be sitting here
for no reason at all, except, perhaps,
she likes to see how strong you are
and the color of your eyes.
Maybe this isn't heaven but near
to something like it,
more like love coming up in elevators
and nothing to think about, except, O God,
you love her now and it makes no difference
if it isn't spring. All seasons are warm
in the warm air
and the brass bed is always there.

If you've done something
and the cops get you afterwards, you
can't remember the place again,
away from cops and streets—
it's all unreal—
the warm air, a dream
that couldn't save you now.
No one would care
to hear about it,
it would be heaven
far away, dark and no music,
not even a girl there.

HOMESTEAD

This house rises into a metallic sky,
a brilliant iron lake under its porticos,
under its balconies and watch towers multiplied
beyond reason and (one, two, three, four) exact calculation.
An institution for the blind,
a sailors' rest (home from the seas)
not quite, but the specific hiding place where John
McCumber Bluethorne, millionaire, sleeps (falls asleep)
after a dozen cocktails.
                    Expects to die
in the inevitable stronghold for his nerves and tissues.
The bright machinery that was his mind
falls silent.
                    His factories (men in the street
crying against him and the quick rifles of the State Militia
are quiet now)
                    Here is the last retreat.
The legend of his wives, his children safe,
locked in iron waters.
                         His mind, fallen inward, stirs no more,
only the house rises;
count the bricks, the stones
and estimate their power
against wind and rain, time and dissolution.

O METAPHYSICAL HEAD

The Man was forever haunted by his head,
this John Brown's body head—
John Brown's body lies—
John Brown's body lies—
John Brown's body lies—
its head goes marching on—
triumphant, bowing to its friends,
lost in a crowd, then bright as dawn
found again, shining through street,
laughing, happy by God, drunk, merry old head,
two cocktails and a bottle of champagne
lighting the dark corners in its brain.

A taxi. Home. O metaphysical head,
the world is too small for it,
barefooted, naked in a bedroom. Bed.
It is awake, remembering, thinking:
I have seen this head too often,
this too-familiar head, yet it changes, changes. . . .
I have seen this young Caesar head
rising above a summer hill, bland and omnipotent,
to meet its love, to see her rise
to this head and with closing eyes
and open lips drinking
the head down until
its brain enters her body
and its will
becomes her will.

And now, the head goes rolling down the hill
(uxorious head),
rolls into darkness, sleeps:
grows large in dreams, serene, awful,
becomes God, opens its mighty lips
crying, Let there be light
in this dream. Let all
women who have not worshiped
this head come naked and ashamed before it
suffering their little children
to come unto it.
Pity for little children,
conceived in sin,
not fathered by this head
but from the needs
of other men.

Awake again, rising from the dream
into the bedroom, eyelids closed,
the head lost in space,
fixed in ecstatic peace,
senses warm, fluid in the body,
but the head, the winged, haloed head gone,
gone where all godheads go,
singing, Heaven, heaven. . . .
                            No,
found somewhere in a gutter,
pitiful, blind, sallow:
And curious friends examine it,

saying, It shall never rise again,
poor fellow.

Put it away.
It hurts us.
Poor fellow,
no words were made to say
how sad we feel. An ugly head—
see what's become of John—
we're sorry, but we must be moving on.

The head gone. Irrevocably gone,
no longer magnificent, the speaker of the word,
divine, exalted, tilting backward in a barber's chair,
august, revered,
floating above a glass-topped desk,
making its power heard
roaring into a telephone,
then brisk, attentive,
meeting its clients and its creditors,
then finally tired, meditating restfully
on the flat bosoms of its stenographers,
on the undetermined virginity of its stenographers.

There would be no offices for headless men,
no girls, nor wives,
only the subway entrances where one may stand
unseeing (almost unseen)
with right arm raised, the index finger of the hand

pointing where the head had been,
the left hand catching pennies.

John Brown's body goes
begging underground
John Brown's body—
No one would dare look at the creature;
it could stand,
a monument for years,
headless, quiet,
forever catching pennies
in its hand.

THE MEDIUM

Spirits rousing out of air—
they are here and shut between
gasps of time that dead men share
with the graveyard and the bell
that swings their bones with music down . . .
and down . . . down . . .
where cold Caesar fell
open-eyed.
                I knew a man
who fed his wits with such as these
to guard himself from tall, dark streets
where women's flesh grew white and trees
were frozen in an iron square. . . .

And on him came a caravan
of noises that went through his veins. . . .

He smiled at ghosts, then took a bride
from old, green Egypt, for her breath
filled his lungs with ancient prayer,
till he too closed his lips and died.

HAGEN

Hagen is dead.
His girl remembers
his quick, bright head,
his well-washed hands
and his lean fingers
and how his cough stained
her bedroom floor.

He'd cough the moon
and a gallon of stars
red as fire torn
from a hundred wars.

All that could cure him
were "faith, hope and charity"—
she couldn't pay his
doctor bills
(and he wouldn't take pity
from her, nor tears).
There'd be no money
in the wills
he'd leave if he lived
a thousand years.

Hagen is dead.
All you can do with him
is dig up his coffin and
look at him there:

he wouldn't be changed much—
he looked like that anyway
and he'd still have
neat, red hair
and a quick, bright head.
That's all you can do.
Hagen is dead.

THE SAILOR

An albatross goes flapping high
As a shadow in the sky,
Far away and far astern,
Following and following
Like a song you used to sing
But you can't remember how
All the words went, nor the turn
Of the melody and now
Only half a tune and rhyme
Circles in the brain and yet
It's a thing you can't forget—
Following you all the time.

An albatross is like a girl
Who is picked up late at night
In the street, or anywhere,
And she'll let you stroke her hair
Till the cloth of night turns pale;
Then she'll kiss you, more or less
Like a fainting half-caress—
But she's always far away,
Far and almost out of sight,
Always like a drifting bird,
Like the song you used to sing
That you wish you never heard,
Following and following
All astern of men and ships
Following.

And what I say
Tastes like bilge against my lips.

Boy, when a man dies, shipmates toss
His body to the albatross.

PRISONER'S SONG

O Mary's lovelier than anything that grows
out of spring trees that stir
April when my mind goes
around and over her.

I love her more than skies bright with the wind and sun
and all my thoughts arise
to travel, one by one,
into her lips and eyes.

She shuts me in her; she holds all my blood and brain
under her lock and key.
Christ! I'm in jail again—
she'll never let me free.

Sometimes, my blind dreams float far—like a wanderer
I go away, remote;
then I return to her
with panic in my throat.

INTERIOR: THE SUBURBS

There is no rest for the mind
in a small house. It moves, looking for God
with a mysterious eye fixed on the bed,
into a cracked egg at breakfast,
looking for glory in an armchair,
or simply noting the facts of life
in a fly asleep upon the ceiling.
The mind, sunk in quiet places
(like old heroes), sleeps no more
but walks abroad in a slouch hat
performing adultery at violent street corners,
then trembling, returns,
sadly directs its mysterious eye
into a coffee cup—there is no rest—
for there are many miles to walk in the small house,
traveling past the same chairs, the same tables,
the same glassy portraits on the walls,
flowing into darkness.

There is no victory in the mind
but desperate valor
shattering the four walls,
disintegrating human love
until the iron-lidded, mysterious eye
(lowered carefully with the frail body

under churchyard gardens)
stares upward, luminous, inevitable,
piercing solar magnitudes
on a fine morning.

MCALPIN GARFINKEL, POET

It is enough for me to tremble,
my vital organs directed toward the sun,
toward the stars,
trembling.

It is better for me to stand at street corners
staring at women, seeing their bodies flowering
like new continents, hills warm in sunshine and
long deep rivers
(even as I am,
trembling)
than to be nothing, to fade away in grass and stone.

It is better for me to believe nothing
than to be nothing,
better for me
not to fight, to let cops and truck drivers
crash through my brains, trample my entrails,
O let me cry out my rage against millions,
carry my remains to the President,
up the steps of the White House
to be deodorized by the Department of Justice
and the Secretary of State,
thenceforth expunged
from the Congressional Record.
But I shall be intact,
no word spoken,

like laughter in my mother's womb, a pointless joke
with no beginning and no end.

And if you hear me crying: My God, my God, my God,
down streets and alleys,
I am merely trembling (afraid, my God, my God,
to be nothing, to fade away
in grass, in stone).

O MORS AETERNA

Be for a little while eternal,
singing with all the songs in your body
but making no sound.

The Rose of Sharon singing in an old city
was eternal suddenly
for a little while.

And the mountains fell away
and the city sank into earth again
and the voices of dead men came from the ground
crying, Incest and poverty and murder
(all in the many dead years
that had sent them into the earth)
but now rising, crying against the world
and mortal sun and moon and stars,
against life and the masters
in purple victories, clothed with iron wars.

For a little while
the Rose of Sharon sang eternally
until the city came around her again
and there was no sound.

II: NO RETREAT

STANZAS FOR MY DAUGHTER

Tell her I love
                she will remember me
always, for she
is of my tissues made;
                     she will remember
these streets where the moon's shade
falls and my shadow mingles
with shadows sprung
from a midnight tree.

Tell her I love that I
am neither in earth nor sky,
stone nor cloud,
but only this
walled garden she knows well
and which her body is.

Her eyes alone shall make
me blossom for her sake;
contained within her, all
my days shall flower or die,
birthday or funeral
concealed where no man's eye
finds me unless she says:
He is my flesh and I
am what he was.

Live beyond hope,
               beyond October trees

spent with fire, these
ministers of false Spring

                    making our bodies stir

with spurious flowering
under snow that covers
hope and hopeful lovers
and fades in timeless seas.

Live beyond hope, my care
that makes a prison for your eyes (and hair
golden as autumn grass
swept by the morning sun)
for you shall walk with praise
when all my ways are run.

Take all my love, but spend
such love to build your mind
'gainst hope that leaves behind
my winter night and snow
falling at the year's end.

Tell her I know

                  that living is too long
for our love to endure;
the tenuous and strong
web of time (outlasting
girls and men—love's rapid signature
of hand and lip and eye)
gleams as if wires were strung
across a sunset sky.

Tell her that girls and men
are shadows on the grass
where time's four seasons pass;
tell her that I have seen

                 O many a nervous queen
of girls (Madonna, glorious
white-towered goddess) fade
while walking in noon's shade,
separate limbs and foreheads bright,
now dim, anonymous. . . .

Tell her I love

        to make these words a song
with her careful lips,

            O bride,
Spring and bridegroom at your side,
save them for the deep and long
silences when northstar light
perishes down quicksilver steep
walls of flesh where love and death
make a counterfeit of sleep.

Take this wreath to celebrate
union of the fire and rain,
bone and tissue.

           Sleep, O bride,
for the waking limbs divide
into separate walls again.

Tell her that flesh is spirited
into earth:
                    this wreath is grown
from black bronze roots to weave a crown
for the death mask and the head
fixed with its metallic smile
upward where generations climb
making garlands of their own
out of iron and of stone.

EMERSON: LAST DAYS AT CONCORD

Enter America at Concord's bridge,
true marriage of the east and west, Brahma
whose lips nurse at my veins.

        Where was the green brass cannon
sunken in churchyards after the shots were fired?
Listen, the world is sleeping and the noise
coils in thunder where Dover's beach
shall wake no more
      and the Indian ocean
pours its blood into the sun when evening's tide
uncovers bones upon the shore.

        Cut me a frock coat, for the oversoul
lies naked: parts, limbs exposed
within a broken coffin. O light that stirs in dust
as eastwind darkens nightfall into rain.

        Where are your lips, hands,
   Brahma?
What was the name, your name or mine?

        Come, friend,
we shall walk in the west orchard drinking russet wine,
kiss daisies where the transcendental tree
(look how the death worm feeds upon its roots)
shelters our love and fiery blossoms fall in Plato's vineyard.

I have carried the world in my brain, have seen its heroes
diminish,
                 saw oceans, continents dissolve in sunlight
on Concord window sills:

                 Are you my friend?
Then here's my secret; I have forgotten
all friends and the words that joined my lips to theirs.
Better to keep faith
                 and believe
no one. Better to be a patriot disowning
this land. Give back America to sunlight, wind and rain;
set sail for India from Concord's bridge,
leap to the quarter-deck where our Columbus
once more commands his ships.
                           Is that a storm in the sky?
And are these apples ripe? I grew this orchard to be a paradise
this side of Eden.

BIRTHDAY IN APRIL

This is the day that I began; this is New Year's
in the terse calendar that opens with my name.
April and south winds in the sky repeat the same
rhythm and the identical body sleeps, hears
Spring at morning waking the same trees that always
wear the sun on slender branches that somehow rise
out of dark streets curved downward at night and men's eyes
cannot discern the roots coiled and unwinding under doors and hallways.

It is not the season but inevitable
return of seasons that destroys the days, the hours
fixed in a man's brain and builds them new again: flowers
and grass covering a ruined city. And full
of these quick seasons, I retrace the day my breath
first issued toward my third decade. Let stones, spires, earth, O Trinity,
      answer death.

PRAISE TO JOHN SKELTON

Praise to John Skelton and
his naked, sinewy rhyme:
the frosty bitten seed
furrowed from his right hand—
root, trunk and branches speed
to flower in our time.

John Skelton, laureate,
doctor divinity,
stripped grandeur from the great
who towered in simony—
uncloaked the cardinal
and Wolsey's skeleton
sloughed lace and crook and pall,
thighbone and carrion,
meet for the carousel!

Skull and charred ribs disclose
how the worm eats the rose,
how the worm, jew'led and fat,
sits with a mitred hat,
eats at the king's right side:
sing loud *Magnificat!*

John Skelton, laureate,
whose sun has risen late
never to close its eye
in our eternity,

opened the lips that preach
virtue in English speech,
the ragged adder's tongue,
sharp, deep and venomous
iron and mirth,
then tart and ruddy song
heard when spring's morning wakes
April whose blossom shakes
birds over earth.

Here is no epitaph—
wreathed coffin, yew and hearse,
poet, to sink your verse
in burial again:
for these lines celebrate
your quick, immortal state:
body, hands, lips and eyes
speak metered gold.

Amen.

AND OF COLUMBUS

Columbus is remembered by young men
who walk the world at night in street-walled prisons:
Where is my country? Why do I return
at midnight to a moonlit, inland ocean
whose waves beat as a heart beats in my side?

Is the return to these receding shores
the end of earth, fallen to deep-sea traffic,
the end of all things?

The cities that coil upward
from sumac bush and sand flow into grass:
roofs, towers mingle
with roots and the bodies of men who died
in foreign wars.

      Columbus who believed his own miracles,
conquered his India, oceans, mermaids, golden savages—
where was his country?

      It was a small stone room at night
where a man walked over the world and seasons merged
in darkness. And time echoes time saying: Columbus no more,
no more Columbus. He is a vanished cloud in the sky
where stars move toward the sun.

And in Havana under the Southern Cross, all that is his
is where his bones lie.

SALVOS FOR RANDOLPH BOURNE

O Bitterness never spoken, the death mask etched in silver,
the dark limbs rolled in lead where the shallow grave conceals
despair: the image of a large head, forward, devouring
the collarbone. No general in brass over it and no
conquering angel kneels.

This was the end:
                    there were no firing squads,
no City Hall Nathan Hale with a bronze cord at his throat
speaking of lives and his country where a hundred million lives
rose, wavered, shattered like an invisible sea coiling
against a rock (no longer there) but sunken
into a shoreline of weeds and sand.

Only a small room and a million words to be written before midnight
against poverty and idiot death like the gray face of Emerson
fading in New England winter twilight; the hard face vanishing
in snow, the passionately soft words issuing from the mouth.
Listen to the rock, the oracle no longer there!

To be the last American, an embryo coiled in a test tube,
to be a fixed and paralytic smile cocked upward to the clouds,
to see friends and enemies depart (around the corner)
their sticks and smart fedoras bright in sunlight,
to be or not to be Hamlet, the Prince of Wales,
or last week's *New Republic;*
to be death delicately walking between chimney pots on Eighth Street,
possibly this is best to be
                    or not to be.

III: CHORUS FOR SURVIVAL

CHORUS FOR SURVIVAL

1

Tell us that love
        returns,
O Hymen, sing
In every hour that burns
After the midnight hour
In darkness here.
        Wake with thy song
The antique smiling year,
Always thy axis turning to restore
The Greek dawn breaking
On Aegean seas.
        Break here
The silent wave upon the shore
In dreams to darkness-driven memories;
Wake with thy song,
Tell us to wake and sing—
Midnight and starlight night are always long
For the impatient young.
Open gray skies and fling
Thy yellow veil, the sun,
        down city streets
Where tireless seasons run,
Speed here October, our retarded spring,
Daylight and green
Live forests blossoming:

The wave-washed rock in embers glowing red,
Wake even here,
                            till climbing overhead,
Window and cornice on steel branches bear
Fire of morning from another spring.

Wake with thy song
                            time-darkened waters
That have not reached their end
Westward to India, passage through storm,
Bearing the image of a Grecian bride,
Eyes like cornflowers staring at our side,
The blue flame lighting darkness in the shade
Of trees knee-deep in grass
At summer's tide. . . .
Only our lips recall
That she was beautiful:
                            the pure
Alcestis memory of a kiss,
                            the violet-
Scented breast, the virginal
Breathing light in sunlit air;
Handclasp remembers hand,
                            quick limbs enthrall
Entwining limbs, the nervous, flexible,
Growing green grapevine,
                            until the blood
Flows into sleep and blood is wine.

This is thy memory, America,
The tenuous marriage of disunited blood,

Captain and slave one bed,
                        in dust until the wind
Stirs dust to live again . . .
                        and walking here,
Conquered and conqueror
(The apple blossoms white in midnight hair).

Wake with thy song
Even in death (they sleep like death)
Men in the wilderness
(The night is long),
                        breaking through forests of a foreign land,
Sell and move on.
Westward we follow to an unknown star
And shall not come again the way we came.

Tell us that love
                returns
After the midnight hour
In darkness here,
Season of iron cities against the sky,
The cold room where I write my signature
Toward my survival in the waning year:
Winter and frost, each day revolves to night,
The longer night that brings a short tomorrow
Of middle age in dark, divided faces,
In faces that I know too well, my own
Face staring likeness in the mirror
Beyond the hour of death or hope or doom;
When doors swing wide upon an empty room,

Window and door open to empty air
Echo in darkness of the lost frontier.

Wake with thy song
                    the voices
Of men who cannot sleep:
                              We count our losses
In decimals of time, the ten per cent
Of what we hope: To let:
                            the naked bed, the folding chair,
Space for the body motionless in air,
Permit survival if we stand alone.
Voiceless we smile; we are not violent.

And from these places
On the abyss of loss,
                         the steel-edged towers
Pierce the moon, the sun:
Look where Atlantis leaves forgotten traces,
Empire of empty houses under seas.

This is thy heritage, America,
Scaffold of iron deep in stone.
                              Destroy the ruins,
This is the place; wreck here and build again.

Tell us that love
                    returns,
Not soft nor kind,
But like a crystal turning in the mind,

Light where the body is:
                        thy limbs are fire
Walking alive among the ancient trees,
The ruined town, cathedral wall, church spire.

Say love, though always young,
Remembers these . . .
                        place, house we entered
And shall not return. . . .
                        Spirit that outlives time
To join our hands in love,
                        do you remember
Serpent and dove, the wild rose and the thorn,
Blossom and leaf in secret flowering
Read in a book of broken prophecies?

Wake with thy song
                (I speak a difficult and treacherous tongue
That was not made for wedding song or carol;
Measure my dwindling shadow on the wall,
Wait for the silence when my lips are gone
That say:
                Though night is long, this bitter hour wakes
And is not sterile).

Wake here
                Atlantis under hard blue skies,
Thy Indian Summer bride is like the spring
Roof-tree in light ·
                thy blossoming
In fire to love returns.

2

Down traffic signals on Park Avenue,
down chromium light imperfect past revealed
in a museum, heart of reality within a dream,
enter New York,
                    the city in a mirror
of Rome, and the calm faces like our own,
even the cracked cheekbone and hollowed eye,
the look of power and sadness and disunion:

   And they were clever
   as we are clever now, eating the heart
   until the breast rang hollow and the remains
   were set on end, secure:
   Hail Caesar, God, erect, the man in stone.
   There in the circus where they stared: the terror:
   the cry for bread
                    and dark sky closed above them.

Apollo's fluid arm embracing shadows
of Asia fallen by Scamander's side,
Athens, the urn, Greek bride of quietness,
descending,
                    turn to see the quickened head
fading in dust . . . the silent legion tread
in tremulous air at Riverside, Grant's Tomb.

The Muse grows old, her lips a quarter-smile
toward death in ruins: there, the black stallion

the horse of poetry, black over white,
the dance in quietness, museum twilight
theirs, forever falling. . . .

Through windows east, the city leans, brick, steel,
deep-banked and floating Chinese Wall looms over
dockyard and river tenement, the poor.

Mirror the city of electric star
light into light
                 on sleepless, quiet faces
less real than statues of the thing they were?
the open hand upon each empty breast?

New York closed into Rome, Rome into Egypt,
Cosmopolis, and only darkness there.

3

Waking from sleep we heard the Great Lakes' tide,
clear spray in wind, white blossoming in dark
night bloom, the city's heat behind us, rolling back
miles westward over plains.
                     Only the sound
of tide, the water leaping these shores,
the lake in wind and in trees over us, the voices
rising in spray, the white tide breaking.

Came Pere Marquette down rivers to the sea,
the inland ocean, bright in wilderness,
sumac and pine.

"Earn heaven for this earth, and iron-blue sky,
the fire-green leaf in the stilled waters—
water, air, fire in my hand, my veins these rivers
flowing to the cross whose flower is man;
the holy tree, blood-red with fruit, the resurrection
waking in this land.
Spring here God's arch, and choir singing praise
through pine and maple crucifix—
                              the forest
trembling with light: O fiery bough."
                              The Eucharist in snow,
death's supper underground and the long winter
under foreign stars.

4

Ask no return for love that's given
embracing mistress, wife or friend,
                              ask no return:
on this deep earth or in pale heaven,
awake and spend
hands, lips, and eyes in love,
in darkness burn,
                    the limbs entwined until the soul ascend.

Ask no return of seasons gone:
the fire of autumn and the first hour of spring,
the short bough blossoming
through city windows when night's done,
when fears adjourn
                    backward in memory where all loves end

in self again, again the inward tree
growing against the heart
and no heart free.
From love that sleeps behind each eye
in double symmetry
                    ask no return,
even in enmity, look! I shall take your hand;
nor can our limbs disjoin in separate ways again,
walking, even at night on foreign land
through houses open to the wind, through cold and rain,
waking alive, meet, kiss and understand.

5

Under the stone I saw them flow,
express Times Square at five o'clock,
eyes set in darkness, trampling down
all under, limbs and bodies driven
in crowds, crowds over crowds, the street
exit in starlight and dark air
to empty rooms, to empty arms,

wallpaper gardens flowering there,
error and loss upon the walls.

I saw each man who rode alone
prepare for sleep in deeper sleep
and there to ride, sightless, unknown,
to darkness that no day recalls.
Riderless home, shoulder to head,
feet on concrete and steel to ride
Times Square at morning and repeat
tomorrow's five o'clock in crowds
(red light and green for speed) descend,
break entrance home to love or hate
(I read the answer at the door)

the destination marked "Return,
no stop till here; this is the end."

6

They found him sitting in a chair:
continual and rigid ease
poured downward through his lips and heart,
entered the lungs and spread until
paralysis possessed his knees.

The evanescent liquid still
bubbling overflows the glass
and no one hears the telephone

ringing while friends and strangers pass.
(Call taxis, wake the coroner,
police; the young ex-millionaire
is dead.) Examine unpaid bills,
insurance blanks and checks unfold
from refuse in a right-hand drawer
to read before the body's cold,

Lifelike, resembling what we were,
erect, alert the sun-tanned head:
polo or golf this afternoon?
And night, the country club or bar?

—drink down to end all poverty,
two millions gone,
                              and stir no more.

Because I know his kind too well,
his face is mine, and the release
of energy that spent his blood
is no certificate of peace,
but like a first shot heard in war.

And not for him, nor you, nor me
that safe oblivion, that cure
to make our lives intact: immure
old debts and keep old friends.

Even in death, my lips the same
whisper at midnight through the door

and through storm-breaking hemisphere,
rise at that hour and hear my name.

7

Through streets where crooked Wicklow flows
I saw a man with broken nose:
His venomous eyes turned full on me
And cursed the ancient poverty
That scarred his limbs and mired his clothes.

O cursed, wind-driven poverty
That breaks the man and mires his clothes.

Beyond the street, beyond the town,
Rose hill and tree and sea and down:
O drear and shadowy green ash tree,
O hills that neither sleep nor rest
But are like waves in that dark sea
That rides the wind, nor'east, nor'west,

O cursed, wind-driven poverty!

Below the hill, below the town,
Deep, whispering voices everywhere
Break quiet in the morning air
And mount the skies to pierce the sun.

I saw the naked, cowering man
Shrink in the midnight of his eye,

There to eat bitterness within,
And close the door and hide the sin
That made his withering heart run dry.
O venomous, dark, unceasing eye
That turned on street and town and me,
Between the waves of hill and sea
Until his eyelid closed the sky.

    The rain-rilled, shaken, green ash tree
    Spread roots to gather him and me
    In downward pull of earth that drains
    The blood that empties through men's veins
    Under the churchyard, under stone
    Until the body lies alone
    And will not wake: nor wind, nor sky
    Bring sunlight into morning air
    And breathe disquiet everywhere
    Into the heart of hill and town.

O heart whose heart is like my own
And not to rest or sleep but climb
Wearily out of earth again
To feed again that venomous eye
That is the manhood of my time,
Whether at home or Wicklow town.
This is my street to walk again,
O cursed, wind-driven poverty,

                I hear the coming of the rain.

8

Praise to the great, but do not enter where they go:
Caesar and Homer, peace where laurels lie
in tombs not mine, discover prince and poet,
de Medici and Messer Aretino,
six feet of man, silks, velvet, cheerful eyes
restored by Titian on a summer morning,
truth's likeness large under Venetian skies.

Then read my portrait and my signature,
image and line, nervous, erect, the linen
clean, head, shoulders leaning over
the naked hand in light, but darkness near,
the darkness after sleep beyond the room,
the canvas on the wall.

Does no one hear
me through dark and quiet, hear the invisible
footfall on the stair?
The flexible body breathing midnight air:
peace under the deep sheltering green rooftree
secure as any Roman ancestor
unearthed in stone and pale the moss-grown head
whose name lived well in brass and is well dead.

Better to be alive, my name unknown,
only the words I write, the clothes I wear
remain my own. Better to feel
this round earth under me, each hour gone,

where I cannot return,
yet always in my blood, my heart reveal
those transient streets where I have walked alone,
saying, I am the tall world's enemy,
a shadow crossing field and street and floor.
Even these words disquiet limbs recall;
truth's in the luminous image as the door
revolving closes and my day is done.

If lies you love, preserve me on this wall
and read immortal lips that speak no more.

9

"The voyage crossed, the firmament one star,
New found New England, home:

>   Now meet me there
In Concord's orchard where the apple bough
Swings over shoulder at the windowpane
In the green season. . . .

>   Wake my limbs again
Adam-Ralph Emerson, the first man here;
Eden, the gate unlatched, this place my own.

And I have seen the world, heard the lark
    climbing
His golden sinuous music in dark air,
That speech unknown but to the sublest ear
Echo through morning over St. Paul's dome,

After a year's travel Emerson recrosses the Atlantic and is back home in Concord, 1833.

He recalls London.

Wing following through April's hemisphere,
Not less familiar now than earth at home:
England, the colosseum of great minds.

Under deep trees, the bright-eyed mariner,
Coleridge, speaking and the music gone:
Miraculous white hair, the oracle
Voice descending, flowing on,

Knowing, perhaps, that I would understand:
Me, in a vision, under visionary eyes,
My pale, frail body and the profile spare,
Visible the wedding guest who must depart,
Must go like youth before the day is done,
Saying 'good-by' and clasp an aged hand.

Perhaps he knew, perhaps he saw. . . .

                                    Perhaps Carlyle
Read something in my veins.

                            We are a little mad
The Emersons, blood thin but deep and the quick
        body given

Mary, "the
aunt of
genius,"
speaks.

To God at bedtime, clipped within the spirit
In sleep, in prayers, the candle lit at dark
In homage to the sun.
Dissolve the body and the light is gone:
The stars expire and angels lose their glory,
The vertebrae within a nest of quiet

Between the sheets to fear the wind that stirs
Cypress and willow over us. . . .

                              Essential
I, the boy, the curious scientific dreaming eye
Fixed on the landscape ash tree, elm,
And rippling grass like water at low tide:
Trees' branches spars of Salem's ships that rode
Jewel-edged at sunset into Asia's side,
Her night our noon, her noonday our tomorrow,
The tropic desert silence under snow. . . .

                              Lyceum
Lectures at the hearth at home, and in the fire
        there,
My boyhood saw   The Emerson
Greek islands floating over Harvard Square: family fireside.
Homer, the blind head sleeping
In celestial seas;
Everett, the voice, asking whose lips were these
Come out of time to breathe our native air?
State House, the fallen stone Acropolis. . . .
And at my hearth, the family Lyceum:
Feed the soul's sepulture, they said, and hear
Dante the Florentine who walked to heaven,
Spiring in golden cages out of hell
To hail unearthly love, the Beatrice
Lady and bride,
                    spirit on the last hill
Of that high world,
                    O Paradiso!
61

And the last desire
Turned in a crystal image on the stair:
More beautiful than dress that angels wear
Was hers, whose waking limbs were cloaked with fire.

Read Thomas Gray, the graveyard nightingale,
The cold rhyme out of season, raven-dark
November-piercing death at April's core:
Love, fame, Cromwell or Milton sleep at last
In dust that circles at the cottage door. . . .
Worship and heresy: God's food, the devil's meat,
Black cloth and ashes where I sit to eat—

The rejection
of the ministry
and Calvinism.

To be divine
                    (and through my heart great good-
        ness flows)
To walk in India at a Concord shrine.

            Bitter the thinking man who sees
            The careful millionaire, the red frontier
            In city walls closed; and the hot mills pour
            Iron for guns, starvation, war:
            To know too well, to think too long:

The bitter hours into seasons pass
Until the soul fills up,
Breaks, scatters backward into that better time
        that never was.

We are alive this hour and survive:

Then, walk with me alone an orchard mile
Into the twilight end of Concord days,
Know in my face the acquiescent smile,
Dissension always deepest in mild gaze
To look down darkness toward the trembling light—

Lights out! and the globe broken, and with hot
    irons
Put out both mine eyes?,
Still gaze toward music where the light
Was and the song:

       Swing chariot philomel in midnight skies!
Broken, yet not unheard.
                Say in my heart I am
That angry ancient legend of a bird
Who walked alive
          eating the ashes of his funeral urn,
Alive to walk until the memory fails
In clapboard lecture halls.

    O my America,
And not to speak of you except in praise,
The midland ocean at my heart,
Thou art Atlantis risen from the seas,
Bride of the Indian Summer and the corn,
The mountain forest, slow, unwinding plain:
The many footed cities at thy side. . . .

I am thy husband to divorce thee never:
Never-forever is a long, long time

Prince Arthur in the Tower: No more the eyes of youth.

The last memory of Europe.

Phoenix.

63

For faith in blindness and the memory gone.

This place an orchard and no roads,
Yet every step I take shall be my own
Till houses fall in houses, cities fall:
Still floats the wedding caul, the oversoul,
My name the hydrographic written on
This stone that crumbles with the garden wall.

    Cheerful, the actual smile is permanent,
    I turn my head always to face the sun."

IV: FORTUNE FOR MIRABEL

FORTUNE FOR MIRABEL

1

Tell, tell our fortune, Mirabel,
Shuffle the pack and cut
Cards spread face upward on the carpet
Over the faded green sweet and violet pastures:
The hourglass, time, the blonde girl and brunette.
Give us good cards tonight: the faces
Beautiful and new—and love, Mirabel,
The pink heart pierced and the great round yellow sun;
We shall be rich tonight: laurels for fame,
The goldmine falling from your right hand,
And O the lute and ribbons and the harp!

—Not the unopened letter nor the blind eye,
Nor the fire card bright as war flowing through Spain,
Nor the lightning card, troopship in storm,
Nor the quick arrow pointing nowhere to the sky.
Not now tonight and not the spotted devil,
The faithless dancing psychiatric patient,
Who wept, always the lover, not the man,
Sold the pawn ticket—not tonight, Mirabel,
Not the deep cypress vista and the urn,
The kidnaped ten-year-old, the head
In pear tree branches and one delicate frosted hand
On the back stairs.

—Nor the green island card that means go home
To the dark house with the gas shut off
Where morning papers drop to the floor,
The milkman passes and the landlord waits—not these tonight.

But the bridal card in white, pale blossoms in yellow air,
New homes unlocked, unwept,
The great good fortune sun card shining down.
Is it love, Mirabel, behind the pearly gates?
This last card? Or the black faceless end
Behind each card, the laurels hidden, the dancer dead,
Tonight over and gray light glancing
On tired, powerless sleeping breasts and arms?
Mirabel: Good morning.

2

It was in sunlit evening, Mirabel,
I saw your face, pale and withdrawn,
The green eyes lighting the deeper, greener shade,
Sparrow and poplar shadow on the lawn,
And gray hair, Mirabel, coifed with black lace
Within a silver veil:
Mint leaf and scent of roses on the air,
And the old promise of the skies beyond the hedge
Of that septennial moon which closes summer.

"Mirabel, Mirabel, tell us our misfortunes," cried the birds.
"We have charmed you into the garden from door and street:

Where are your cards?
                        Nor age nor youth nor pride
Should stop you now; we should hear the worst;
Even the Fates, despoiled by what they know,
Think of themselves as young, as beautiful
As you—artless and shy,
Flushed with their graces in a mirrored room."
But you had grown sulky and would not speak,
And the reddening light of evening poured at your feet.

And silence came (I believe you turned your head),

I saw a figure stand beneath a tree—
Had he been nailed to bare branches before lightning struck?
"He is not Christ," I said,
"The crown he wears is not a crown of thorns;
It is a wheel such as fools wear on dancing holidays;
Your cards and prophecies
Have wakened him from the garden of the dead.
I hear him singing, 'Nothing but love,' still more,
Grape leaf and hellebore
Grow from the glittering tendrils of his hair."

As the storm's darkness fell,
I heard you whispering your beads,
And I knew before darkness came you were in his arms;
There was a black book in your hand
That had dropped to the ground.
"Tell, tell misfortunes," cried the birds,

"There is more to tell";
And where you had walked, I saw the fiery wheel.

3

Mirabel, the sinful Irish, when they die,
Always return to Eire:
There none is lonely; the cold rain beats
In waves against the soul, and moss-green
Angels in deserted gardens stare through the rain
And slowly lift their wings.
                              It is where
The sirens, whisky-weeping old women, comb gray hair,
Beg for a penny to curse the world,
To wail, to sing. O it is where
Wandering blue tapers burn through fog
Among frail girls clasping their guilty lovers:
White limbs in the moon's light in an empty house,
Eden's sin in rags by day, and at night
The serpent uncoils his desires.

                         It is on that dark
Island, Mirabel, where the last wheel turns,
Where cards fly into the wind, good fortune and bad,
Speed into storms that ride behind pale suns.
Mirabel, your eyes are lidless, raise your face:
Look at the birds; the swallows wheel like bats
And have nothing to say
While rooks and ravens circle the cold sky.

Mirabel, the spell is cast, turn where you will,
The purple hills still rise, the blackthorn tree
Tears at your sleeve.

                This is the place
Where the first sight of heaven is a last look at hell;
Perhaps there is sleep before morning, Mirabel.

TWO LETTERS FROM EUROPE

1

It was the wishing castle that had deceived us:
day-spring at midnight song through every window,
linnet and sparrow,
and from each sill the ivy-circled dawn
waking each day into a last tomorrow,
piercing bell-towered tapestries and halls,
as if we could delay, if not forever,
the hour that leaves no choice
and is the sacrifice of our own blood
in gardens floating green beside the river
and rose-lipped entrances through summer walls.

There we had walked together,
brother and sister, friends and lovers;
and where we turned (it always seemed
we had been running away and yet stood still)
the castle suddenly opened its wide doors
where every welcome was a face in tears,
the endless deep embrace of Cybele,
and from that cavern we heard the voice
of an aged man who, rising out of earth,
held in his arms the body of his young daughter:
"O face, dear face,
                    O breast, O golden hair."

2

As flares fell from the sky

                I saw trees' veins
open their withering branches to entwine
the antique shadow of a white-haired, white-limbed man,
and as it spoke, it seemed a hand had lifted
a golden bowl that held September wine:

"Poetry and truth have been my life,
the difficult searching
among rocks, thorns, and all around me
the deceptively innocent gaze
of Nature from the eyes
of a young girl or from the vault
of heaven or from a white rose
staring among the brambles at my feet.
Only the Greeks saw Nature
through the windows of the mind.

I shall no longer tremble, pale as grass,
before the luminous image of what I was,
the young god in a forest of old cities,
breaking through leaf and flower,
through wall and stone,
calling its love to shelter
under its star-reflected breast and loins,
its will, the earth-will, and its blood the dancers
whose fires are lit beyond a moss-grown stair.

Since I have seen the end of a long day
of peace that was the mirror of old wars,
my voice shall echo from another night
and from its tireless, wheeling stars unfold
light within darkness that replies,

                                        more light,
heard from the lips of a last dim, anonymous face,
the child born crying into a naked world."

THE WAKEFUL HOUR

"Pour l'enfant, amoureux de cartes et d'estampes,
L'univers est égal à son vaste appétit.
Ah! que le monde est grand à la clarté des lampes!"
                                        —BAUDELAIRE

I saw the country of the sleepless, glancing eye
Where things resemble life.

                        Even the distant people
Who walk in thin electric mountaintop blue air
Are lifelike here, and over there
Is a valley where slow sheep gaze
At a man's body fallen in grass, and are things seen
As if for the first time and the last,
And are now, as if forever, bright and clear:

The shining husband, straw flower in his lapel,
Enfolds his love's short breast and quickening side,
And beyond the suburb, a white casino rises,
Gleams like a wedding cake and disappears,
And through the park at evening faces are
Wheeling behind plate glass in limousines;
It is a vision of life within motion,
Volition within life
That has no beginning and no end
And is always near.

                        Beneath the floodlit tower clock
A lost child with a sailboat under his arm

Stares at the time. And at his side an old man on a bench
Faces the river where the factories are
Until light fails and a far window opens like a pale wishing star
Blank bedroom walls where two naked lovers quarrel.

In a wakeful hour I almost hear
Noise of lost cattle in a trampled field,
The husband's voice, the laughter of the bride,
Gear-shift of motors through the park,
Boy's cry and factory whistle,
The scream, the thrust of a body against the wall—
And if one saw them as one might see them in a mirror
Move, dissolve in night and reappear,
That would be life itself and always there.
I have heard that the ancients saw them in a circle
From light to darkness, darkness to light again,
Seen through the branches of a golden tree.

They stand between me and the unseeing, unlearned, unknowledgeable
    world.
I wear them as a man might wear a shield.

TWO MONOLOGUES FROM THE PASSION OF M'PHAIL

1

Do I have to prove I can sell anything?
You can see it in my eyes, the way I brush my hair,
even when I need a drink and can't stop talking.

Do I have to prove it with my two hands and arms,
lifting five hundred pounds above my head,
until the house cheers and something falls,
the platform broken and the lights gone out,
crowds calling for police,
and a child crying for its mother down the aisles?

If the park is beautiful and the day is warm,
I can sell the power in my eyes that makes life grow
where not even one blade of grass has grown before,
that is like sunlight breaking through
darkness in a small room,
that shines and pours and flows,
that is here forever when it is here
and is gone forever as sunlight drops to darkness
when it goes.

I could even teach millions how to sell,
how to own a car and pay the rent,
how to live as though you were living in the sky,

your children happy before they get too old.
If you do it right, you can sell anything,
even your voice and what you think you hear,
even your face on billboards ten feet high,
your youth, your age and what you hate and love,
and it gets sold.

If you can wake up in the morning early,
if you can teach yourself to catch the train,
if you can hang out everything for sale,
if you can say, "I am a man,
I can sell asphalt off the street,
I can sell snowbright
dead women gleaming through shop windows,
or diamond horseshoe naked dancing girls,
or eight hours on my feet,
or twenty years of talk in telephones,
or fifty years behind a desk"—
you need not fail.

If you are strong as I am, you can hear
yourself talking to yourself at night
until your hair turns gray:
"I am God's white-haired boy,
I almost love the way I sell
my lips, my blood, my heart: and leave them there,
and no one else can sell such pity and such glory,
such light, such hope

even down to the last magnificent,
half-forgotten love affair."

Perhaps only I can do it as it should be done,
selling what remains, yet knowing that a last
day will come and a last half-hour,
or five minutes left impossible to sell,
the last more valuable than all the rest.

2

When you are caught breathless in an empty station,
and silence tells you that the train is gone
as though it were something for which
you alone were not prepared,
and yet was here and could not be denied;
when you whisper, "Why was I late, what have I done?"
you know the waiting hour is at your side.

If the time becomes your own, you need not fear it;
if you can tell yourself the hour is not
the thing that takes you when you sit
staring through clinic waiting-room white walls
into the blank blue northern sky
frozen a quarter-mile above the street,
and you are held there by your veins and nerves,
spreading and grasping as a grapevine curves
through the arms and back of
an enameled iron riverside park seat,
you need not think, Why must I wait
until the doctors say:
                    "We have come to lock you up.

It's the psychology of things that has got you down;
if you complain, we shall take care of you
until you know at last you can't escape.

Is your dream
the dream of a child kept after school
made to write a hundred times
what three times seven means,
while in your sleep, before you get the answer,
the blackness fills and swells with pictures
of Technicolor ink-stained butterflies?

Is that ink-blot a tiger
in a bonfire? Are these the spines
of ancient caterpillars?
Is this the shadow of a wild-wood, leaping deer?
Is that what you see, or what you think you see?
Then we can tell you what you are,
what you can do, and what you ought to be,
as though your life were written down in court,
your name the last word on a questionnaire.
There is nothing private that we do not know;
you can't deny these figures on a chart
that follow you no matter where you go.
Each zero is an open, sleepless eye
piercing the hidden chambers of the heart,
and if you fail, or if you kill yourself,
we shall know why."

It is when the waiting forces you to stop
in stillness that you wish would not return
that you say, "I am not the same as other men;

I must live to wake beyond the fears of hope
into an hour that does not quite arrive. . . ."

And in that quiet, lost in space, almost remember
the difficult, new-born creature you once were,
in love with all the wonders of the world,
seeing a girl step, white and glittering as a fountain,
into cool evening air,
knowing you could not touch her,
nor dare to still the floating, flawless motion
of that pale dress above its glancing knees,
brief as the sight of sun on Easter morning
dancing its joy of earth and spring and heaven
over the sleeping bodies of men in cities
and between the branches of the tallest trees.

It is then you tell yourself:
"Everything I live for is not quite lost,"
even if you've waited someplace far too long:
if you can't call it peace, you call it rest;
if you can't call it luck, you call it fate,
you then know that when anything goes wrong,
perhaps it also happened in the past.

You light a cigarette, you carefully
blow out the match.

                              You know again you have to wait.

MUTUM EST PICTURA POEMA

"Do not curse me:

               It was my friend
who framed these sketches
of dying tulips in a glass,
of potted rosetrees, and a street scene
that might be Alexandria or Venice
or New Orleans or perhaps an unfamiliar
noon-struck vision of an overnight hotel
at Niagara Falls.

It was she
who locked my spirit within white,
staring, mausoleum walls.

It was not I
who was unthoughtful or unkind,
but she who sought to justify
love by another name,
to call it art and reverence and fame,
and not that living thing,
voiceless and blind,
that prays for solace in an empty bed.

I had been a good child always, had obeyed
teacher, father, mother;
if she could have taken me for what I was,
and if I could have said,
Open my heart: it is the place where hell is,

you would not be looking at these pastels
nor at that sleeping girl who seems to wear
at her right side a mutilated hand,
nor at these pale and drifting water-lilies."

DAEMON AND LECTERN
AND A LIFE-SIZE MIRROR

For God's sake, do not explain that picture
of the bright-haired girl on a diamond black horse,
nor the stilled eyes of imperishable Greek ladies
carefully undressing before a life-size mirror.

Let us be glad that we cannot discover
daemon or child who made them, that these realities
of delight and beauty at their imperfect source
are indiscreet, if not indecent, subjects for any lecture.

THE POSTMAN'S BELL IS ANSWERED
EVERYWHERE

God and the devil in these letters,
stored in tin trunks, tossed in wastebaskets,
or ticketed away in office files:
love, hate and business, mimeographed sheets, circulars,
bills of lading, official communiques,
accounts rendered, even the anonymous letter says,
Do not forget.

And in that long list: Dean Swift to Stella,
Walpole to Hannah More, Carlyle to Jane.
And what were Caesar's Gallic Wars other than letters
of credit for future empire?

                 Do not forget me,
I shall wear laurels to face the world;
you shall remember the head in bronze,
profile on coin.

As the bell rings, here is the morning paper and more letters:
the postdate, 10 P.M.: "It is an effort
for me to write; I have grown older.
I have two daughters and a son and business prospers,
but my hair is white. Why can't we meet for lunch?
It has been a long time since we met;
I doubt if you would know me, if you glanced quickly
at my overcoat and hat and saw them vanish
in a crowded street. . . ."

Or at another door, ". . . O you must not forget
you held me in your arms, while the small room
trembled in darkness; do you recall the slender, violet
dawn between the trees next morning through the park?
Since I'm a woman, how can I unlearn
the arts of love within a single hour;
how can I close my eyes before a mirror,
believe I am not wanted, that hands, lips, breast
are merely deeper shadows behind the door
where all is dark? . . ."

Or, "Forgive me if I intrude, the dream I had
last night was of your face; it was a child's face,
wreathed with the sun's hair, or pale in moonlight,
more of a child than woman, it followed me
wherever I looked, pierced everything I saw,
proved that you could not leave me, that I am always
at your side. . . ."

Or, "I alone am responsible for my own death" or,
"I am White, Christian, Unmarried, 21," or, "I am happy to accept
your invitation," or, "Remember that evening at the Savoy-Plaza,"
or, "It was I who saw the fall of France."

As letters are put aside, another bell
rings in another day; it is, perhaps, not too late to remember
the words that leave you naked in their sight,
the warning, "You have not forgotten me;
these lines were written by an unseen hand
twelve hours ago, do not reply at this address, these are the last
words I shall write."

V: NEW POEMS: THE GARDEN AND THE CITY

A TEMPTATION OF ODYSSEUS

I know that island:
It is a garden, and beyond hedge and sea wall—
It is a singing forest of young girls,
Their faces roses, their hands, arms, shoulders
Foam against rocks, white as the throats
Of lilies, girls stepping out of trees,
Walking, as if created out of air,
From willow branches and waterfalls,
From springs and fountains.

There I could whisper,
Look at the languorous one, that creature
Who shakes the sun's hair out of her eyes;
She is the light that moves
Among dark ferns and grasses. She has opened her lips
And is about to sing. I doubt if
What is heard is music—but O that pale
Forehead and lovely shoulder.

And with her is one
Who has midnight in her glances,
Nubian quiet in her eyes where a man enters,
Is drawn, is held as a child is carried,
Sleeping, within four corners of a dream,
The room where ash and laurel lift their branches,
And shades of those who killed the Minotaur
Beckon and disappear.

That island is a place
Famous for the noises of its waves,
Bird-calls, cave-echoes, storms of ancient sky
Which are transmuted into the sound
Of girlish voices, a spell that entrances
The lonely man (God help him) lost at sea.
Even learned mariners and snow-bearded captains
Have not been immune—who did not trouble
To hear the meaning of words or score;
They welcomed lightning and reef,
Shipwreck and shallows, the naked beach
Where the tropical island is a threshold
Into dawn.

It was true
I stopped my ears against the singing,
But the secret is: I had closed my eyes
To keep the island out of heart, hope, mind:
If I heard anything it was the shrill
Of peacocks.

It was then I knew
That all my men would leave me; the ship was gone,
They were free to enjoy the quickened dark, the rescue,
The wild embraces, the songs, the shrieks, the laughter.
It was useless to threaten them
With chains and galleys and the loss of home.
They were free of the lot of those who die in irons;
The Fates had given them a sailors' choice
That is reserved for the young, the gay,

The ignorant whose blood is wine,
Whose bones are salt for sirens.

   I know that island
As if it were the Zodiac at night
Shining within the palm of my right hand.

HOMAGE TO CIRCE

Lady, the glass you lift has sleep's bright fever in it,
Amber and floating peace within a place
Where he who drinks cannot expect to hear
The throbbing of the skies, the watchful flight
Of wings above his head, nor guide sea-traffic
Through a crowded street.
                  Lion, dog, or swine,
He is a cheerful patient,
Ready to give till he has nothing left to take—
It is the fever that inspires his rosy look.

Lady, you have that rosy look,
Lips shaped as though about to speak, to sing;
Is the fever hot or cold? Do eyelids close forever
In the depths of the fever,
And through the sky-borne arches do sea-bells ring?
Whose are those delicate arms that reach to hold us
Through plate-glass halls where glittering in mid-air
The body rests, and each revolving mirror
Reflects a sleeping mongrel at his ease?
Is this the place of miraculous hotels,
The forest feast embracing us with branches
Where all the rosiest ladies turn to trees?

Lady, your precious glass cannot tell time,
But is of an hour that is forever gone;
Even for your sake its light will not return,
Nor farewells spoken with a gliding smile—

Lady, our journey has outstepped your spell,
We have destinations beyond your kind distractions:
We have passed, are passing
To the sober shores of hell;
It is cold among the waters of the dead,
A less feverish province than the animal kingdom
That is always at your side.

                       We have found no haven,
And our long night has just begun,
Yet over Hades something opens like a sky;
Perhaps in darkness we are closer to the sun—
There is no misfortune as we wave "Good-by."

HAUNTED ODYSSEUS: THE LAST TESTAMENT

       Do you see them? I mean the Dead:
They have come back again; I feel them walking
About the room, and a face has entered
Through that closed door.

                I have seen them rising
In fountains out of rocks, the unwept slain,
The green moon-shadow on white breasts and thighs,
And heard their raining voices in the wind;
I saw pale hair
Floating in golden waves against the dark,
I saw hands reaching toward invisible fruit
That once had dropped through summer's heat
Above them.

        This was in their country,
The Palace of the Dead, snow falling as crystals fall
From a dark sky. I heard the sound
Of thick waters moving against rocks, the shore;
Their houses had been burned by fires
Greater than the sun: there were blackened walls,
Each hearth, each portal
Open in ruins to gray sleet.
I saw a ledge, a handrail and no stair,
Only the deeper darkness and the depth
Of another corridor or pit.

                    Then from the shadows
I saw a wavering light and heard,
"My dear, my hope, my love," the light
Spoke to me, and I said, "Mother,
What dream, what evil sent you among these ruins,
Lost as a child is lost
In the mischances of love and war?"

                            "Death," she replied,
"I am spirit only: all that was flesh
Is fallen into earth or consumed by fire—
The human fate that waits for all of us
Has little patience for those grown delicate and old.
Then my transparent veins released my spirit
To walk among the unwary, the undone.
I am the vision that speaks to you in sleep;
You cannot hold my shade within your arms,
Even my slightest breath has turned to frost;
It dare not touch you—this is my last
Good night."

                    Where the light spoke a star
Shone through the portal and was gone.
My brain clouded with tears; I had forgotten
To ask her of the way back to life.
Then I remembered that a shade
Had stepped between us,
The blinded foreigner from Thebes
Who stood as if a tree grew at my side;
I heard the sound of leaves above my head,
And saw a black bough pointed east.

Perhaps my escape
Was almost fortuitous. And now at winter's midnight
The Dead are here whispering through snow;
They crowd upon me
Between walls of a room or in a quiet street:
"*Mea culpa, mea culpa,*" from earth or ceiling,
"The fault is our fault, *mea culpa*, we are to blame;
We are wanderers of Hell in every city,
The faithless, the unloved.
If at the last turn of the wheel in Heaven
The first cause of our fate is in the stars,
We shall wait for you behind an open door
And in your shadow as you walk the stairs."

VENUS AND THE LUTE-PLAYER

                    That young man—
Thin face, dark eyes in shadow, the blue Venetian
Skies and water below the balcony,
Seen where horizon
Falls into distance over his left shoulder—
Makes music with an art that angels sing.
Such songs have power to wake the moon,
Unveil her sleep and draw her from the skies
To walk with him as though she were his bride,
Her light glancing loggia, stairway, stone,
Floating, reflected beneath waters of the canals.

                    Madrigals,
Songs are flames of Monteverdi
Within the lute, golden in fire as darkness
Turns to day, and rain to fountains
Dancing in the sun.

                    And one might think
Such vernal arts would capture Venus,
But there is no likeness to his music in her eyes;
She stares and beckons as though her radiance
Alone were summer's noon, as though she said:
"My hairs are golden wires, and what I am
Has been compared to fruits, flowers, vines,
Jewels in the earth,
And the silver motion of the sea—I have no need
Of music nor music's art. I am eternal

Even beyond the sight of artful men.
My presence wakes or sleeps, silent, unsought
Within a darkened room; I need not rise or speak.
I, the world's mistress, remain indifferent
To strings that tremble, to reeds that blow.

                        I am what you seek,
And all you need to know."

IN GEORGE SAND'S GARDEN

Someone remarked:
"The indecorous lady is no longer there,
Pursued by young and all too faithful lovers;
The print of small feet and the hooves of deer or 'satyrs'
Is not to be discerned among the grasses."
Nor are there signs, among bruised leaves, torn branches,
Of the encounter, almost breathless, and the fall,
As if into earth's center, when the subtle movement
Of the sea is distinctly felt and promises of love
Are overheard among ferns, vines and a sheltering wall
Of roses.

She was neither all heat nor cold:
Her fires were gathered from the autumnal light
Of the moon in her first quarter who seems to walk
Between and above the trees in early evening—
And are as public as the moon,
As quickly turned from cloud-washed gold to silver.
What changeable colors, fragrances, riverlike sounds
And glances entered and vanished
In the illusion of her eyes, of limbs and shoulder,
Of dress and nakedness, and in the green-reflected
Disquiet of her hair.

Even when one saw her
Stride like a man, heard her voice crack,
And knew her veins were filled with a fluid that was not blood,
Was deftly poured, as in a wineglass, for many palates

To taste its salt, to count the beating of her heart
Against the lips, and knew her action
Had less art in it than the command of mind and will—
Even then, among her "rash *sorties*," the perversions
Of taste, mind, feeling, a less and more
Than human spirit caused a trembling of the leaves,
Sat for the camera, smoking a cigar,
And at the center of a room, draped in soiled linen,
Advised by unpaid physicians and counselors-at-law,
Remained serene.

        Was this, then,
"The Eternal Feminine"? life in short death that "makes us
What we were before"? a metamorphosis
From sex to sex?—so she was read,
Gazed at, applauded, and half, but only half
Forgotten.

        And in her garden, serenity
Is in the summer afternoon, in *"nature morte,"*
The trimmed lawn, the white and empty marble garden seat,
In skies that open with a blue and vacant stare.
In the sundial, in the distant vista through the trees,
Is the lady there?

ELIZABETH AT THE PIANO

It is memory speaking, preternaturally clear,
Awake, remote: the piano playing
Through the dark midwinter afternoon,
The string-filled music at four o'clock,
Chopin, Mozart, Suppé.
$\qquad\qquad$ What I remember
Of that lilac-breathing house
Are flames against dark windows,
And beyond the curtained door
A young girl seated at the square piano.

$\qquad\qquad$ Listen: I hear
The walking metronome: one, two, one, two,
Then the minuet. It is the practice hour,
The pendulum swinging between the walls,
Upstairs and down.
$\qquad\qquad$ There is the smell
Of wet lath, of rain-darkened plaster.

Behind the house the wintry lilac forest,
And behind the coals in the grate
The winter sunset smolders.
$\qquad\qquad$ Is that flame
The sunset breaking through the fire?
One can almost hear the pendulum walk the stairs,
The lonely footfall, then the minuet.

Awake, remote, the house stands in gray—
Clouded brick, leaning through gray midwinter sunset air,

The firelight failing behind the curtained door.
And at the piano in the shadowed room
The dust-filled metronome
Clicks: it is the practice hour.

                             And is that face,
The sunset glancing through darkness
Over white and rose, and caught within
Moonlight of yellow hair, her face?
Is the child there?

Faintly, the minuet—or is that sound a bell
Ringing, unanswered, or someone calling
A child's name down the street?
The house looms, then fades in the wind;
It has begun to snow, the piano is glazed with sleet,
Then frost; it is snowing everywhere.

THE ALPHABET FOR JOANNA

In a child's garden of drawings I came upon a book:
A for the serpent's Apple and wide-winged Albatross;
B was for Bull, Bible and Bell, and "to Be" spoken
In a voice out of a cloud. And there was C, the Cat, coiled in a Chair,
And three-headed Cerberus, the Dog, who stands for D,
Who ate his Dinner in the Dream's shadow
Where water flows behind an unopened Door;
E for the faceless Egg, Easter with dancing suns,
And E for Ermines worn by kings on cards
And guilty, light-haired, pale-eyed player queens.
F for the Fish and Fox, the hooked and trapped,
Floundering and fleet in Flood and over Field,
And G for Grapes and Grass growing beyond a Gate
Where Hills are always H and Heaven and H's are
Horns blowing from Hell's Hearth and fiery Hedges
On Halloweens.

        Then I, thin "I,"
Myself walking in mirrors, wide-eyed, an Island
In green glass, speechless and half asleep
Before J, the Judge, in a white collar and a black nightgown
Where Jubal sings beneath a Judas-tree.

                K for the King in Kilts,
The gay Kinghorn who sits with a captured princess on his Knee;
L, the caged Lion, from the age of gold
Stares at gray Lazarus risen from the dead
While M, the Man, measures night's Mountains in the Moon,

103

And N glides near with a great spider's Net
That catches flies where numbed Napoleon stands
In a lead soldier's blackened uniform.

O is the Ocean and the Ocarina, the sea and wind,
Orion in the sky and the Oriole's breast;
P is the Pole where weather turns to ice,
And P's are Palaces where Princes stalk at noon
To meet their Queens in Q's that stand in line
To answer Questions: "Is R the Rain?
Or is it Reindeer flying through snow, or Raphael,
Angel who spoke aloud to Adam?"

                               Swifter than S in the Snake,
And brighter than Snake's eyes is Saturn
Burning above the T-crossed earth where T is
The night-wandering Tapir and Targets pierced with darts,
Where Tambourines spin and dance under the bear,
Ursa, and U is Unicorn, the Visitor, V, at night
To lonely Virgins.

              W is the Way, the hidden Walk
Beyond the Wall; X, the unknown, the blue-lighted
X-Ray that shows the skeleton in a darkened glass,
And Y, the Year that runs long June to short December
While Z, the Zodiac, turns its wheel in heaven.

As the book closes, the difficult numerals begin
And multiply in twos and threes and fours,
Yet the alphabet remains where all things live—
The world through open windows and wide doors.

SEASCAPE AT EVENING: CAPE ANN

What is that sound, what is that blue and golden light
Between the rocks, running through grasses,
And at night walking beneath Orion and the moon?
Its colors are in cornflower and honeysuckle,
And wherever one turns, morning or evening,
It is the sea.

               It is the presence
Everywhere: the invisible weeping face
Between the branches of the trees, the ancient
Wild sound between sun and moon, the Doric
Greek return of rock and island:
Voice of the sisters who walk the tide,
Who speak the fortunes of the dead
In salt wind lifting
The pale arms of the sea.

               Even the innocent
Blue flower at our feet stares at us
Through the bright glass of sea and sky,
Speaks to us of the veined rock and the gray forest
Hidden in roots and moss: what does it say
Of lives that have turned to stone?
I hear their voices in the wind, in the waves, in the cries
Of the white-breasted and great-winged
Birds of the sea.

VOICES OF HEROES

Overheard in a Churchyard Dedicated
to the Memory of 1776

"The cemetery stone New England autumn
Restores health to our voices,
Even our faces
Seem to reappear through gliding mist that gathers
In an unshuttered, moonlit, empty room.
We were the heroes, O wives, mothers, daughters!
Of war that lighted fires
Within these shores.

Open our graves: you will find nothing there
Unlike our common clay
That blows away,
Or mixed with water serves to build a wall;
But you might well imagine
That earth and air
Are relics of the True, Original Cross,
And that the trampled grass
Holds the imprint of Adam's image on this small hill—
Or you might say,
'Because their bones lie here,
The bleak earth glows with sunlight from their eyes;
These are the heroes
And their voices speak among us at their will.'

Yet too much praise leaves much unsaid:

Even in death we were, somehow, more human,
Moving among the shades of things we loved or hated,
Clasping the shadows of pretty girls, of restless women,
Or quarreling with a landlord,
Or gazing with regret at empty bottles,
Or shouldering old rifles,
Or for an hundred years (since we were freed from labor)
Playing at cards with a distrusted neighbor.
It is not true that we were always sad,
Or like evil, unquiet dead misspent our fury
Among cries of death at night in winter storms—
But the earthly spirit that fed our hearts had gone,
Gone with the vanished hope of richer farms,
Or brighter towns, or countless money;
We had learned that there were no stakes to be won,
That the unnamed, vital essence returned to God.

Now that another war flames in the east
(We can see its fires reflected in the sky
And there are more than rumors in the air)
Remember that we died fighting for what you are—
Better to die
Than to sit watching the world die,
Better to sleep and learn at last
That terror and loss
Have not utterly destroyed us,
That even our naked shades
Still looked and talked like men—
That when we wake,
A little courage has earned our right to speak.

Remember that old wars remain unfinished,
That men fail, fall and are replenished
As grass grows over earth, our names forgotten,
Or misread, misspelled in ivy-covered stone
With wreaths above our graves in summer's green—
Is that blaze the blaze of lightning from a cloud?
Is that noise the coming of October rain?
We do not fear them; we know that flesh is mortal
And in a world at war, only the wars live on."

THE BLUE WATERFALL

(Hokusai 1760–1849)

From green heaven to green earth
The blue waterfall: colors
Of spring and summer:
The green-breathing fern and moss
Within pale-lipped rock
And falling water: trees'
Branches golden in light
Against blue water:

                "O river
Of heaven to earth," is a prayer
Said by leaves of the forest,
"Give us your blessing, rain
Into the rivers under
The bridge where the sky
Flows."
        Look, it is there
In the sun; it is the fountain
Wall of blue fires.
            As it is
In heaven, so it is
On earth where the golden goddess
Walks: her face is the sun.

Hokusai, the print-maker,
Stepped out of night

At the fiery center
Of the dragon's eye.

                His eye
Is the eye of the dragon, his hand is
Of sword and sun: it speaks
The will of the goddess: earth, air
And light, her will the blue fountain
Where the woodcutter kneels
To drink of the waters
That are always wine.

                    The green
Earth is awake, the blue waterfall
Is where the goddess
Walks at noon.

              Hokusai
Is there: his brush made
The fountain, his brush made the prayer
Of the leaves in the forest.
It is always noon.

THE NIGHT-WALKER

Artemis, Artemis: there is fading
Glory in her net, in the silver
Curtain that falls from sky to street.

Above roof and cornice her face
Returns behind the silver rain;
The ancient huntress walks across night.

Sleepless, she warns and charms,
Sees the new age fallen out of the old,
New ruins where elder cities stood. Indifferent

Is she to these; she has come to warn us
That her pale life, her sterile mountains
Have outlived wars. Her arrows are unspent,

They are still falling in silver light
Above, within the city, their shadows deeper
Than any shelter on the scarred walks of earth.

She is not of our being: she is wandering
Artemis who endures beyond life, she is
The light behind a cloud and has deceived
The unwary into an immoderate love of death.

SPYGLASS

This a spyglass: it
Reads the deepest waters,
Reads the weather, it tells
The time of day, it pierces
Fog and cloud, it searches out
The moon, the sun; it is
A lidless eye, open at morning
And alive at night.

Touch it: even blind senses
Know its ceaseless stare,
How it looks inward to
The dark and how it gazes
Through the outer air.

                              It is
The spyglass: it is now
Directed across the plain,
Over a broken bridge, into
The forest, through elm and pine,
Oak leaf and briar, a side of
Rock, a glint of water, the ivy
Vine—careful, the glass is very
Powerful, one can scarcely
Hold it—it has seen
Something that moves, that runs,
Throws itself flat,
Leaps, circles as if shot,

Stands upright, dives, yet cannot
Escape the glass. It is
Running, it has tripped, is
Running, it has grown smaller
Than its shadow, it has lost
Its shadow among the branches,
Among the leaves. The glass
Has caught its face; it is
What we thought it was, not quite
An animal—its pelt is fluttering
In rags—not quite a god;
It is not hard to know what
Its strange features mean;
It falls again; it is
The disappearing man.

THE CAGE OF VOICES

Hear them, hear them—all
Of them are back again:
The schoolmaster and the boys
And girls, the white-haired
Middle-aged red face, the faces
Of the young, laughing, laughing,
Laughing behind closed doors,
Or on stairs, or in the hall.
Hear them, they know, they tell
All you have done, where
You have been and why;
All are talking, talking,
Chattering in the next room.

This is more than a dream:
It is something that is awake
Within a dream; it wakes
And follows you out of bed,
Out of the room, out of the house
And down the street. Hear
Them through an open window,
An open door. Stand in the street
And the shop windows look
At your eyes and hands and what
You wear. They know the secret.

That little girl with the pale
Sharp face and small green eye

Could, if you ask her, tell
Everything: her lips are moving,
She talks in whispers, but an hour
Later, she is a sibyl
Speaking through the walls—
She is merely one of them.
Hear them: they have disguised
Their voices to make you think
They are talking of someone else,
Not you, nor yours, but of
Some other death, some other life;
Yet, if you listen closely,
Closely as when the ear discerns
The stirring of the wind
Within a yellow leaf, or is
Almost certain of a crying
Whisper in the rain—

                              you shall hear
Them speak as voices call
In sleep; they have returned
And you must hear.

THE LADDER AND THE VINE

Basalt and coral and gray rock:
This is the portal
Where the dreams walk,
The feathered queen
Who weeps, whose voice is like
The chattering of leaves,
The bird-beaked king
Who glides through dark
Among night-flowering lotus.

          Cypress and olive bloom there,
          Green within green,
          Green within rock and moss
          And the green shadow,
          Quick as a snake
          Behind a child's face
          Smiling in a mirror.
          Look, look into the forest
          Where the sleeper stirs,
          Sighs in the moonless dark
          As the portal closes,
          Green within green, O fastness
          Of the shade and vine.

It is there one feels
The night wind of Avernus,
The darkening silver
Deep-echoing well water

Closing above uplifted hands
And floating hair.
There is no volition
Of hand or shoulder
Within the well,
The faces veiled in green
And shade and vine:
The wheel-eyed Centaur
Embraces sleeping Psyche
Whose lips and folded wings
Breathe within stone.

It is there one hears
The dreams: "We are the voices
Of sleep and shadow
At the shuttered window,
The question heard
At the closed door
Heartbeat and echo
Between trial and answer,
'What is man?' said in the tongue
Of the serpent, 'What is flesh?
What is spirit
That when it leaves the body
Casts no shadow in the sun,
Yet flames in darkness
Of the outer air?' "

"Within the well is our shelter,"
Say the dreams, "all, all

Are sleeping here, body and spirit
Sleeping, and beyond us
Lies the desert where no one comes,
Who dares to enter it?"

And from that waste a voice
Like the voice of Jacob
Cries, "I have seen angels
Rise and fall and call upon me
As though on a ladder
In a pillar of light;
One is wreathed in ashes
From the city of evil,
And the other, fair as the sun,
Stepped from a cloud
As though its will
Were the will of God."

It was in the desert
And from outer darkness
That the third angel came,
Green as the spotted serpent
Clothed in brass.
It was Jacob's spirit
That wrestled self against self
In the eclipse of sun and moon,
That tore and maimed and bled
Till the voice of light was heard
And the desert flowered
And the temple stood.

Basalt and coral and gray rock:
The tongue of the serpent
Is the key
Of both trial and answer.
After the chattering of leaves
Is stilled, heartbeat and echo;
The portal closes and the sleeper wakes,
Turns toward the desert
In the gold eye of heaven.

STATUE IN THE SQUARE

As though I stood at the center of the world,
Gray walls of stone and sky circled the figure
Of bronze-green Dante with its laureled head
Among thorned branches of a winter tree:
"Speak to it," said a voice,
"Speak to that stern, sad, staring face
Which seems to lean out of another time
To this late afternoon, the more than human
Pity and grace as though its light had poured
From sunless skies into this windswept place
Over gray street, park bench and city square.

"Speak to it," said the voice, "even at the hour
When the clock's eye opens upon men at war;
These streets, unlighted windows and black boughs
Are not unfamiliar to its quiet gaze.
Where the ground trembled and grasses wept
It has mused upon lost friends and enemies,
It has witnessed and foreseen
Blood on this earth that feeds the roots of trees
And pierced the world into another season
Of day beyond winter, spring, summer, fall
Held in the golden, dream-filled look of a young girl,
Beyond the passion of the grave,
Beyond the last embrace of earth or love."

As I heard the voice, I saw the dark face vanish,
Yet knew its presence in the darker air,

The hand-clasped book, the cloak, the bough, the laurel:
Even though earth fail us and street and city gone,
We shall know that figure and its fiery star
Rising behind the ceaseless sun and moon.

THE WOMAN WHO DISAPPROVED
OF MUSIC AT THE BAR

We heard her speaking of Chinese musicians
And of the house she sold in Westchester;
She said that she could not live there forever
Waiting for things to happen in the mind
Until Martinis entered on a tray,
Or the doorbell rang, or footsteps on the stair
When one was sure the musicians had returned—
Better to live without doctors, lawyers, friends—
And relatives might ask too many questions—
Better to sell everything and move away:
"If I could have said, 'Musicans are gentlemen;
They have asked permission
To rehearse *Persephone* on the front lawn,
Their viols and brasses
Are heard discreetly as the cries, the laughter,
Bird-song and weeping
Of a lonely child who wanders underground,
Her grief, the shadowy spray of maidenhair,
Her joy, the violet in April grasses,'
I could have hired them to play for guests at dinner,
Their music served with sherbets, iced Chianti,
Tinkling behind a plaster cast of Dante,
Echoes, farewells, Stravinsky quieted
Among white roses in a vase,
Trembling between the stems of stained wineglasses.

"It would have been difficult for me to prove
That they were Chinese;
They had come at night, I turned my face away
To the darkness of the wall beside my bed.
I knew that they were there, quite as one knows
That death is in a room, or birth, or love,
Wailing and sighing;
I heard them play
Such music that is heard among the trees,
The sightless music, gong and waterfall,
And I knew that there were faces in the room,
The stone-carved smiling lips and empty eyes
Until I said like someone in a dream,
'I have locked the door: you cannot use my house
As though it were a room in a hotel—
You must let me sleep—
Even if you kill me, the police will come:
There will be blood upon the floor,
A broken chair, torn sheets and footprints in the garden,
And no one shall escape.'

If they had promised
Not to return, I would have stayed,
Have looked each neighbor in the eye and said,
'I have not lied:
There were twenty men among the hollyhocks,
Among sweet peas and oleanders,
And at twelve o'clock they came into my room,
Barefooted, in rags and smelling of the East
As though the earth had opened where they walked.

I was careful not to let them know my name;
I am not responsible for what you may have heard.' "

When the woman left us, one could not have known
That two weeks later
She would actually disappear,
Her phone disconnected, the top-flight suite for rent,
That perhaps the musicians had returned,
Even in the city.
One could not prove that they had followed her.

POLICE SERGEANT MALONE AND THE
SIX DEAD DRINKERS

"My last job was the case of the Six Dead Drinkers:
It has given me dreams and my work is less efficient,
It has shown me the will of death and I am impatient
At the lack of will among those who choose to die,
Even ill-health is a palpable excuse;
I should have dropped the case.

The men were found in a hotel linen closet,
The sixth with a three-inch rope around his neck,
A college student who pretended to be dead,
A fool who whispered
That all youth dies, that he did not wish to live:
All seasons burned for him in hell, he said—
"Rimbaud, Rimbaud, Rimbaud!"
His breathing corpse was sent to the Polyclinic
Where they brought him to and washed his hands and feet
And offered him the rewards of war and love.

I wrote the first report: it was 'heart-failure,'
Bodies intact and clean, no stains are visible
On wall or floor—
And the victim (if he chooses the occasion)
May wear a judge's gown, or a dinner jacket,
Or the tonneau of a State Department car—
After the police and the mayor are photographed,
Newsmen are always glad to be satisfied.

If the case had been one of gas-house disappearances,
Or a run of phone-booth murders,
Or a Papal Count with an Islip heiress in a lost sedan,
I would have let
The Fairview psychiatrist reclaim the bodies,
For he had said what no one should forget:

                  'These men are not quite gone,
They have merely sunk or drifted past their prime:
Each body is a little overweight,
Regular exercise would have done it no great harm;
There is alcoholic content in its blood,
This one is deaf, the other is half-blind,
Another has a scar on its right side
And still another lacks an index finger,
Which is sad, but each can be beautifully repaired,
Therapy works wonders for such common ills.
They could weave baskets, or model images in clay,
Dye wool, or trace a pattern on a loom,
Or even calcimine the clinic walls—
Each could be salvaged and each could earn
A minimum of fifty cents a day.'

But I had my way; I restored them as they were,
Each in the closet as though sitting in a bar,
Friendly, about to speak:
One looked like a schoolteacher with a glass eye,
Another like a teller in a bank,
Another like a sailor, reefed and spent
On an East River barge, one like a millionaire

Who had been reported missing for a week;
And the last with his smile rolled upward to the ceiling
Might have been a correspondent in the First World War.

Like one possessed, I sat down among them to hear them talk,
The door closed quietly and the night was dark:
I felt the cold, stilled air against my face,
I knew the danger, I knew how deeply
Sleep flows among the dead, how straight, how far
The unseen distance falls, my body shaking
And held upon a narrow ledge.

I awoke to throbbing airdromes in the sky,
The nurse above me said:

                    'You must lie quiet,
You have been telling me secrets for days, for hours,
Throat scorched, lips black and your tongue burning;
You have told them all, there is nothing more to say.'

But even as I woke, I could not stop:
There were years more to tell
Of misspent childhoods in the sun at Santa Fe,
Or ten days with a duchess on the Matterhorn,
Or minute views of the Louvre from Eiffel Tower,
Bomb-scares in Jermyn Street, tear-gas in Wilhelmstrasse,
Male sleeping beauty contests at Marseille—
All, all were there,
Even to the least detail,
Memories of girls with the Indian Ocean in their eyes,

And night-breathing oleander in dark hair,
Words flowing from the lips that could not keep still—
Were there five men in that place, or six, or seven
Whispering my life, or theirs?
I did not know,
I knew only that a phosphorescent, blue-lighted river
Coursed through my veins, that I must talk as if forever
Of everything I had done, or hoped to do.

It was no wonder my recovery was slow,
That I enlisted to begin my life again, to leave the city.
I have heard artillery encourages silence among men—
If they sing, dance, shout or whisper, it does not matter,
The guns speak for them and the sirens blow—
The service leaves no mysteries unsolved;
I have volunteered—

        and I am wild to go."

A FOREIGNER COMES TO EARTH ON BOSTON COMMON

In the shadow of Old South Church the turn of spring is
Slow, melancholy rain from eaves and branches:
There is the smell of clay that once had been
Eyes that feared heaven, hair delicate to touch,
Lips that almost parted to drink, to weep, to smile.

                              It is reported
One can hear voices running through the grasses,
And at evening whinnying between brick walls.
There, as rain falls, the text is found:
"Vanity," saith the Preacher, "is a rainbow
Glittering against clouds that are filled with tears,
Fold within fold,
Coral in amber, emerald in amethyst,
And is the arc of that crystal ball which is the world."

                              Sunset discovered
A figure standing between trees and traffic
Unmindful of the dark behind the Common,
Or of approaching night, or of draughts and storms;
He stood as though he felt
The noon of summer in his heart and the sun streaming
Within the veins of his thin arms.

                              One could almost hear
His fingers call the birds,
Striking and straying, as if they tuned a violin,

Invisible strings of music in the air:
"Sister Water, Brother Fire,
Earth and her Seasons whose lips are roses,
Whose breasts are lilies;
Welcome all creatures in flowery dress,
And in thy circle bring pale Bodily Death
Who walks like a woman weeping behind her veils
And gathers the living with her under grass."

                                      Then to him came
A multitude of wrens, the jade-green parakeet,
Wild dove, hawk-sparrow, the flickering
Virginian nightingale, the mothlike Dusty Miller
Flying and fluttering to his knees and shoulders.
When the wings stilled, he began to tell them
Of trees that grew barren at the top,
Of towers that suddenly filled with light, then fell to ashes,
Of the capricious laws of birds and men,
Of the circular blue and golden joys of heaven.

                                After the birds had flown,
Those who saw him spoke of his archaic head,
Thin nostrils, dark face and transparent body
That rose in air through which night gleamed and stirred.

                                   One had heard him say:
"To see the world without profit or grief
One must lean into it as through an open window;
Waterfalls and rocks abound there,
Flowers and vines, meadows of wheat,

White alps and purple valleys—
After that vision, the gray Serpent who drinks the ocean
And eats the heart and mind
Is nothing but a dream."

                                      It was agreed
That what he saw could not resemble Boston:
He had talked of meeting angels in the street,
Of a flaming bush that could not have grown
In Copley Square. Some said it was fortunate
That he did not return; others that birds have not been known
To sing praises of men. It was clear that no one but a saint
Could speak as he did and not have his eyes
Plucked out by nervous crows.

OPERA, OPERA!

What work is that?
An Investigator speaks:

"It had been discovered that lenses
Of opera glasses could not be controlled;
They had been cased in mother-of-pearl
And jewelers called them 'a scientific work of art,'
Glittering to look at in the fluorescent glare
Of a salesman's eye, but when one touched them
The hand became unsteady, and the sight
(If one saw anything at all) became
Unnaturally clear.

            A box-holder reported
That he saw Valkyrie riding through the lens,
That he could count October falling tears
Of Orpheus raining in a painted forest
Through autumn leaves and papier-mâché towers,
Gray twilight billowing in canvas skies;
He said he could almost hear the chiming choirs
Of angels with tinseled hair and violet wings
Who gazed at heaven with mediterranean eyes,
That when the lens
Pierced the asbestos curtain,
At last he knew that something had gone wrong.

            The lens showed Parsifal,
His hairy legs and arms wrapped in a bathrobe:

The box-holder saw the hero stir
Patented headache powders in a cup;
In the Green Room he saw
The woman who was once Eurydice,
Naked as Eve with Adam at her side,
Kiss the reflection of her lips within a mirror.
It was then he noticed that the house was empty,
That the galleries were dark and all the faces gone.
It was as though he had fallen into a cave,
And he felt the invisible shadow of Anubis
Walk through the aisles. He almost wept
And then discovered a nightwatchman
Who unlocked an exit, hailed a cab
And sent him home.

Another victim

Said the lens viewed nothing but history:
Elephants that crossed the Alps in snow,
Winged chandeliers from the Congress of Vienna,
Coiled in smoke, torn volumes
Of civil law and economics,
Rocks among blackened stumps of trees,
Foreshortened deserts and a broken cornice
Where someone carved:
'Voice of the people is the Voice of God—Hail Caesar!'

Another said

That the glasses had been given to a child
Who hoped to see, green as a billiard table
A baseball diamond hidden

In the park, but grew impatient,
Lifted the lens at bedside to the moon
And through a window saw concentric circles
Wheel into a gray sphere with night unrolled behind it;
The boy cried, 'That thing is the face of death,'
The Ram, the Lion, the Archer had disappeared,
Nor could he find his own elusive star.

It was decided
That opera glasses betray the universe,
That the view within the lens was both too near, too far:
If the glasses were a 'a work of art,'
They should be destroyed, but if 'scientific,'
The valuable lenses could be brought
Almost to perfection, refined, repolished for expert use
Among ourselves, among friends and enemies
In restless peace and all-pervading war."

THE BEGGAR ON THE BEACH

"I have not come here to talk;
I have come to sit; I have been transplanted
From the cornerstone of a First National Bank
On a windy street to root myself
In pebbles, shells, and sand;
It is my shadow and not my arm
That holds out its fingers in an empty glove
Which might so easily be mistaken for a hand.

My silence is
The unheard cries of those who swim
Where no raft follows, where sails, masts, funnels
Disappear up-ocean into a wave that travels
Eastward beyond the thin horizon line;
At my left shoulder there is a cloud
That gathers into a storm
On a beach-crowded Sunday afternoon—
The cloud my shadow's twin in the tide's swell
Which churns gold waters into lead and silver
At its will.

Tell me my riddle:
I am not a mirage, but a being in flesh
Born of a sea that has neither
Waves nor shore, nor moon, nor star:
That was my misfortune. Have you a better
Fortune? are you forever young, handsome, rich
In friends? poor in fear? happy in doubt?

Sad in nothing? hopeful in dark?
Is that what you are? Or do you burn
As my veins burn with ceaseless heat?
Whether you answer me or not,
Even at noon, the disguise I wear
Is the body and rags of legless Kronos
Before God walked the sky. Look at me and his shade
Turns boardwalk holidays into a mile
Of broken bottles and twisted iron
Seen through a gray window in the rain.

     Give it your homage,
The shadow is always here. Now you may drop
Your money in my hat."

THE REHEARSAL

Gentlemen, as we take our seats
In the darkened house, let us rehearse
The properties of the Western Theater;
Attention: this is item one,
Cloth of the Sun and Moon; it is
The Firmament, see how it glitters—
Life beyond life on earth, and
Beautiful. It has been praised,
Many regret to close their eyes
Upon it, the eternal skyscape
Which seems to wake at morning,
To burn at noon and to unveil
A silver mask at night. We do not
Hear it and yet its changes are
The Music of the Spheres—

                            so much for that.

What of the others? plant life,
Animal life, the earthly spirits?
Item: a Lock of Gilded Hair
From the Head of Venus, a Tree
Of Poisoned Apples, a Yellow Snake,
A Hebrew Maiden and a Naked Man—
We need not name them, they
Have walked out of the sight
Of God; they share our dark-
Ness. Here is a White Hot
Caldron for the Jew, a Chain

Of Dragons and Hell's Mouth,
And St. Sebastian with a Weeping
Eye—tears? Four Glassy Tears,
Four Kingly Crowns: Russia,
France, Germany, Spain, a Wreath
Of Smoke, all painted on a curtain;
Behind the curtain, the West Wind,
And in the Wind, Three Cries of Beggars,
The Halt, the Maimed, the Blind.

Gentlemen, this is our Gold, our
Inheritance—even the Gibbet,
The Mask of Folly and the Stake,
The Fall from Grace, the Earthly Power—
We cannot sell it, and though
No actors come, we shall wear it
To warm us in the cave, protect
Us from heat on the rocks, from
Dark, from flood, from moving mountains
Among ice, the fire of lightning,
The drifting wilderness of snow.

THE UNWILLING GUEST: AN URBAN DIALOGUE

—How still, how very still the air is
As though it waited, is still waiting
For the clock to strike. Did you see that shadow
Fall behind the clock, behind the white face
Of the dial?

   —No.

—Will you have a drink?

     —No.

—Another cigarette?

    —No.

—If I lift the curtain I can see
Three Spaniards, a Welsh Albino and a Levantine Greek
Drinking their hearts away. One wears
A newly rented evening gown. I can almost
Hear them singing. Did you say something?

       —No.

—That's half the charm of living
In the city. Do you expect to stay here long?

       —No.

—You must remember it is a holiday: the
Coronation of another half-century,
And nearly midnight. The snow is falling lightly,
Carefully drifting, yet the room is very warm:
"You could fancy we were lying
On the beach." Do you want to sing?

         —*No.*

—Do you find the room unnaturally quiet?

            —*No. It*
Is probably trying to think. If anything waits
For something it cannot think.

—You mean it falls apart? But the room is still
Here. You can sit on the table or pace the floor
Or talk.

      —*That is what I meant.*

          —Listen,
Is that a starling behind the chimney-piece? Or water flowing?
I forgot to water the statues in the hall,
The three girls picking flowers, the little ones
Called Morning, Noon and Night. And the large ones,
Father and Mother, who sometimes talk,
Should be fed at once, then covered with a cloth
And put to sleep. One becomes extremely
Domestic if one lives alone.

>   *—That fluttering*
> *Of wings behind the walls could be echoes*
> *Of a blind man playing a violin,*
> *Or is everyone in the city blessed with eyes?*
> *You needn't answer.*

>   —There is a half-domed
> Casement pouring light above us; it is not,
> But looks like a three-quarter moon.
> Would you like to see it?

>   *—No.*

>   —If I open the shades
> You will see layers and layers of freshly cut
> Plate glass, light splintering
> The streets from a million windows.
> And O the people! Everyone talking, laughing, dining out,
> But you cannot hear them. Here is one window
> Filled with dancing couples, and in another
> Four children are playing cards, and in that window
> I think I see a party at a concert:
> The usual pearls and gloves, white shirt fronts,
> Naked shoulders—and minutely printed on a folded playbill
> Held in a woman's hand, *Roméo et Juliette.*
>   And in the windows
> Everything to sell: the latest inventions
> In copper wire, spun brass, guncotton, steel,
> Even uranium, each almost perfect of its kind,
> Sharp, clean, reflecting light—O a million lights,

141

Floodlights out of the dark,
Cross-beamed, white, yellow, red against the sky.
Shall I open our window?

—*No.*

                          —Everything looks
As it has seemed for almost fifty years,
A trifle overbright, but ingenuous, cheerful,
Mindful of holidays: the Alexandrian city.
Do you remember Alexandria?

                          —*No.*
—Pharos?

        —*No.*

            —If I draw the shades
It is as peaceful as Pharos before the tower fell.
But we, of course, are on a different island,
Hearing other rumors, if we choose to hear them,
In the African silence of this room.
Shall I unroll a map? There are rumors
That all cities are fires dropped from the sky
In a curious geography of wars:
This shaded portion of the map was Pharos:
The gods no longer walk there.

                          And across the water
The grape withers and runs over

A mound of thistled grass, and look, the Pillar
Of Cestius is a pyramid of smoke.

                      There is nothing here
That the wind cannot blow away, except the harbors,
Except in the deeper forests perhaps
A cave. If you look too closely, the map is
Like a lecture at a museum
That no one cares to hear. Is that shadow still
Wandering behind the clock? Even as you leave the room,
It is still a temporal hour:
It is excellent weather for a holiday.